HEI

This **[** ... **]**ghts
to thi... ... you
heal and grow.

Disasters affect everyone in different ways, so
your book will be different from everyone
else's. It's yours!

MY NAME IS

_____.

I'M A SURVIVOR.

LIVING-IN SAFETY

You may feel AFRAID.
And that's okay.

There are lots of wonderful things in the
big, wide world. But there are some scary
things, too. Earthquakes, wars, car accidents
and diseases are just a few of them.

Write down some other scary things here:

_____

_____

_____

Here's one survivor's wish:

"I wish I had wings like a dove!
   Then I would fly away and be at rest.
   I would escape to a place far away.
   I would stay out in the desert.
   I would hurry to my place of safety.
   It would be far away from the winds and
   storms I'm facing."

Psalm 55:6–8

4

5

Have you ever had a wish like the survivor's wish.
What is your wish?

All comfort comes
from God. He comforts
us in all our troubles.
Now we can comfort
others when they are in
trouble.

2 Corinthians 1:3–4

Write or draw your wish here.

I wish …

SURVIVAL TIPS:

- Make a plan. Ask a grownup to help you fill out the Emergency Plan on the back of this book. Talk about your emergency plan.

- Pray. You can always talk to God when you are afraid. He can be your place of safety.

- Ask your family to help you put together a home emergency kit which includes: a battery-powered radio and flashlight, food and water.

- If you have a pet, make an emergency plan for them, too, which includes a leash, food, and ID tags.

TAKE ACTION!

- Make up a SURVIVOR SONG.
  Sing your song when you are afraid.

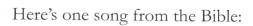

Here's one song from the Bible:

The LORD gives me light and
saves me.
Why should I fear anyone?
The LORD is my place of safety.
Why should I be afraid?

Psalm 27:1

9

ASKING FOR HELP

You may feel POWERLESS.
And that's okay.

It might be hard to tell someone
that you need help. Remember, the
people in your life want to help
you. But they won't know how to
help unless you tell them what you
need, so ... TELL THEM!

Jesus taught us how to ask for God's help.
He said we should pray like this:

Our Father in heaven,
may your name be honored.
May your kingdom come.
May what you want to happen be done
on earth as it is done in heaven.
Give us today our daily bread.
Forgive us our sins,
just as we also have forgiven those who
sin against us.
Keep us from falling into sin when we
are tempted.
Save us from the evil one.

Matthew 6:9–13

Ask God
for what
you need!

12

We can always ask God for help. Make this prayer your own by filling in your words.

The LORD gives me strength. He is like a shield that keeps me safe. My heart trusts in him, and he helps me.

Psalm 28:7

God can be a shield that keeps you safe— like the shell of a turtle keeps it safe.

God, thank you for loving me so much.

Today I feel

_____

because of

_____

_____ .

I need your help. Please

_____

_____

_____

_____ .

Thank you for

_____

_____ .

SURVIVAL TIPS:

• Tell people you know and trust what you need.
Let them know how they can help you.

• Be careful about talking with strangers, though.

• Tell people what you need. Let them know
how they can help you.

TAKE ACTION!

Be a helper. Watch for someone else who needs
help. You can help with small jobs (like washing
clothes or you could read for someone who is
unable to) or big jobs (like repainting a building).
Ask if you can help. It feels great to help!

FEELING COMFORT

You may feel SAD.
And that's okay.

You may miss someone who is gone now. You
may think a lot about how things were before.
You may not know exactly how you feel.

God, you see trouble and sadness.
You take note of it.
You do something about it.

Psalm 10:14

19

Jesus said,

Blessed are those who are sad.
They will be comforted.
Blessed are those who are free of pride.
They will be given the earth.
Blessed are those who are hungry and
thirsty for what is right.
They will be filled.
Blessed are those who show mercy.
They will be shown mercy.
Blessed are those whose hearts are pure.
They will see God.
Blessed are those who make peace.
They will be called sons of God.
Blessed are those who suffer for doing
what is right.
The kingdom of heaven belongs to
them.

Matthew 5:4–10

God uses families and friends to comfort people who are sad. He also comforts people himself!

21

Doing something fun may help you feel better.

Do you like running really fast?
Do you like drawing?
Do you like looking for crazy-looking insects?

Make a list of your five favorite activities.

GREAT THINGS TO DO

SURVIVAL TIPS:

- Tell someone who loves you how you are feeling.

- Tell God about your sadness. Ask him to comfort you. Watch for the ways he does.

- Do something on your
  GREAT THINGS TO DO list.

TAKE ACTION!
Make a SENSE BOX.

1. Get a box.
2. Decorate the box with paint or crayons or anything else that will make it special.
3. Fill the box with things that have good smells, tastes and sounds.
4. When you are sad, get your SENSE BOX out and enjoy some of your favorite things.

LETTING GO

You may feel ANGRY.
And that's okay.

You may feel like life isn't fair.
You may be mad about things you've lost.
You may wish that things were different.

Draw a face that
shows how you
feel here:

GRRRRR

It's okay to be angry, but it's even better to let go of anger. Lots of times we need to forgive someone for something they did that hurt us. Then we can begin to let go of our anger.

Living God's way gives you the power to forgive people and let go of anger.

You are God's chosen people. You are holy and dearly loved. So put on tender mercy and kindness as if they were your clothes. Don't be proud. Be gentle and patient. Put up with each other. Forgive the things you are holding against one another. Forgive, just as the Lord forgave you.

Colossians 3:12–13

Sometimes, you may just need to yell really loudly to get rid of your anger.

Make a **YELLING-TUBE**.
1. Roll this book up like this:

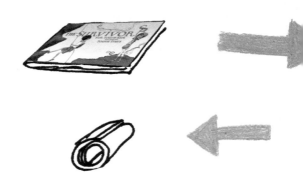

2. Put your mouth up to one end of the tube.
3. Put your hand over the other end of the tube.
4. Take a deep breath.
5. Yell as long and as loudly as you can.

SURVIVAL TIPS:

- Forgive people. Ask God for the power to forgive the people who have hurt you.

- Talk with an adult that you can trust about how to handle your anger.

- Use your Yelling Tube.

TAKE ACTION!

Easy ways to avoid anger:

- Pretend you are someone else. What changes when you see things from another point of view?

- If you are angry, take three deep breaths before you do anything.

- Get enough sleep.

Go forgive!

32

Do not let the sun go down
while you are still angry.

Ephesians 4:26

33

MAKING A CONNECTION

You may feel LONELY.
And that's okay.

You may feel like the world is big and you are
very, very small. You may miss someone you love.
You may be far away from your friends or family.

If you are missing someone, write
the name of that person here.

Write the name so it looks like the person
in some way. Make the name look

fancy or CRaZY or very small or

REALLY BIG.

34

35

God is a father to those
whose fathers have died.
He takes care of women
whose husbands have died.
God gives lonely people
a family.

Psalm 68:5–6

From the very beginning of the world,
God said that it was not good for us
to be alone. You need friends and
family, too!

Be a friend!

36

37

One great way to reach out to people is to write them a note.

You can write

a *thank you* note,

a note of *encouragement*,

an **I miss you** note or

a don't you wish you had a pet giraffe note.

Be creative! The note you write will be a way to connect with someone.

You can connect with Jesus by asking him to teach you to live his way. You can talk to him no matter where you are.

When you become a follower of Jesus, his spirit is with you. Learn about following Jesus by reading the Bible and talking to other people who follow him.

SURVIVAL TIPS:

• Be a friend. Look around you and thank God for the wonderful people living with you.

• Write a note. Reach out and connect with someone.

TAKE ACTION!

Learn to love the people around you.
Love looks like this:

> Love is patient. Love is kind. It does not want what belongs to others. It does not brag. It is not proud. It is not rude. It does not look out for its own interests. It does not easily become angry. It does not keep track of other people's wrongs.
>
> Love is not happy with evil. But it is full of joy when the truth is spoken. It always protects. It always trusts. It always hopes.
>
> It never gives up.
>
> 1 Corinthians 13:4–7

41

MY EMERGENCY PLAN

My name is _____
This is my Emergency Plan.

If there is an emergency, I will go to _____
                                                    (my

My emergency contact person is _____

My contact person will _____
                                    (contact metho
to get in touch with me if there is an emergenc

God is always there to help us in
times of trouble.

Psalm 46:1

42

_____ .

_____ .

place)

_____ .

_____

NOTES:

_____

_____

_____

_____

_____

_____

_____

_____

_____